BLOOMERS

on Pikes Peak

the story of
Julia Archibald Holmes

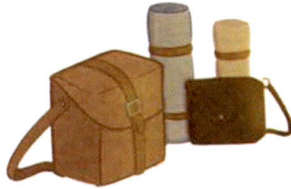

Library of Congress Control Number: 2024920013

Sharon Kizziah-Holmes - Book Design

SOLANDER
PRESS

Published by Solander Press
Springdale, Arkansas

ISBN: 978-1-959548-70-6 (Hardback)
ISBN: 978-1-959548-71-3 (Paperback)
ISBN: 978-1-959548-72-0 (eBook)

Dedication

To Grandmother Clara Urrey Brown, who instilled in me the love for writing in my childhood, and Dusty Richards, whose friendship and inspiring words at a writer's conference reignited my passion for writing as an adult.

Acknowledgements

Thank you, to the South Dakota State Historical Society and History Colorado for your help with this project.

BLOOMERS
on Pikes Peak
the story of
Julia Archibald Holmes

by
Clarissa Willis

illustrated by
Armand Hayes

After a long, hard journey, Julia Archibald Holmes climbed one of the tallest mountains in Colorado. At nineteen years old, she became the first pioneer woman to reach the top of Grand Peak (now known as Pikes Peak).

Julia Archibald was born in Nova Scotia, Canada, on February 15, 1838, to John and Jane Archibald. She was the second of eight children. Raised in a family that challenged societal norms, Julia learned from her parents to stand up for what was right.

When she was ten years old, her family moved to Massachusetts. Her parents were abolitionists. They believed that slavery was wrong and worked to try to stop it.

Julia often sat in her parlor and listened as her father and mother spoke against slavery. Her parents joined many others in protesting the practice in the United States. But soon it became clear that to make a difference they needed to do more than protest and attend rallies.

In 1856, Julia's family made a bold move by leaving Pennsylvania for Kansas. Together, they helped provide shelter to runaway slaves as they traveled north to freedom.

At eighteen, Julia actively participated in the famous Underground Railroad. In Kansas at the time, helping enslaved people escape was against the law. Julia learned that doing the right thing was often hard and dangerous. She and her family faced arrest because of their efforts to help the runaway slaves, but they continued.

The home of Julia's parents became a popular place for other abolitionists to meet.

At a time when women could not vote and did not speak often in public, both Julia and her mother were active participants in these secret meetings in their parlor.

During these meetings, Julia met John H. Holmes of New York. John liked Julia's courage and willingness to speak her mind.

Their friendship grew into love. John proposed, and they were wed in 1857.

Something big happened in 1858. Gold was discovered near Grand Peak (Pikes Peak). The United States had just acquired a large amount of land from Mexico.

This western land (later known as the Colorado Territory) became crowded with those hoping to find gold.

The newly married couple left Kansas
and headed west for the gold mines.
Once again, Julia stood up for herself.
At the time, women wore long skirts
that touched the ground. Many wore hoop skirts that
made walking or riding in a wagon uncomfortable.
Julia wore bloomers on her trip—loosely fitting pants
under a short skirt.

A fellow traveler, Mrs. Robert Middleton, suggested, "If you have a long dress with you, do put it on for the rest of the trip."

Despite criticism, Julia's decision to wear bloomers was another way to show her independence. She wrote in her diary.

"I can't afford to dress to please others; I will not make the journey in long skirts which will confine me to the wagon."

Following the Santa Fe Trail, most of the time, the trip to Colorado was difficult.

There were mountains and deep rivers to cross. People often had to walk in bad weather so the heavy wagons wouldn't sink into the mud.

Each day of the trip, Julia got stronger.
No matter what happened, she kept going.

In her diary, she wrote: "At first, I could not walk over four or five miles without feeling quite weary by persevering and walking as far as I could every day. In a few weeks, I could walk ten miles in the most sultry weather without being exhausted."

The trip was not without problems. Like the men, Julia insisted she be allowed to help guard the wagons at night. The leader of the night guards said no.

She wrote, "I believe women should be afforded the same privileges as men. . . . I think, when it is in our power, we should be willing to share the hardships which fall to men."

Julia and John finally arrived and made camp near the present-day location of Colorado Springs, just below the large mountain known as Grand Peak. They soon gave up the idea of being gold miners.

They decided to climb a mountain instead.
On August 1, 1858, Julia joined her husband
and two other men as they attempted to
climb Grand Peak. Even though it was
summer, the weather changed as they
climbed higher.

Carrying a seventeen-pound backpack, Julia started the difficult climb wearing a short dress, bloomers, moccasins, and a hat.

Even as the weather got colder with each step, Julia did not give up.

Two days later, she wrote in her diary, "We are at the east side of the peak, whose summit looming above our heads at an angle of forty-five degrees is yet two miles away towards the sky."

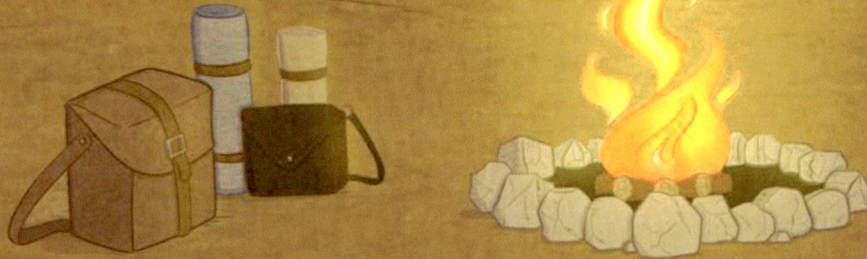

The group decided to continue but left their backpacks behind. For the last part of the trip, they carried only writing materials and basic supplies.

On August 4, 1858, Julia and the others arrived at the top of Grand Peak. Julia sat on a rock at the top and wrote about her dangerous journey.

"I have accomplished the tasks which I marked out for myself. Nearly everyone tried to discourage me from attempting it, but I believed I should succeed, and now, here I am. I would not have missed this glorious sight for anything at all. I am the first woman who has ever stood upon the summit of this mountain and gazed upon this wonderous scene."

Julia and her husband eventually moved to New Mexico, where she taught school and worked as a reporter for the New York Herald Tribune. Later, she moved to Washington, D.C., where she continued to fight for important issues, such as the right for women to vote.

Glossary

Abolitionist: A person who wants to stop or end slavery.

Afforded: Allowed or permitted.

Bloomers: Loose-fitting pants worn by some women in the 1850s.

Confined: Restricted or made to stay in a small space.

Grand Peak: Later named Pikes Peak, it is the tallest mountain in the southern part of the Rocky Mountains.

Hoop skirts: A bell-shaped undergarment worn by women to make their skirts stand out from the body.

Marked out: A phrase used in the 1800s that means setting a goal or making a plan.

Moccasins: A type of footwear made of leather and often worn by indigenous people in North America.

Pan for gold: Gold is found by looking in streams using a pan. A small amount of dirt from the stream is scooped into a pan and then loosened by water.

Persevering: To keep trying, no matter what obstacles one may face.

Santa Fe Trail: A popular route for wagons from Franklin, Missouri, to Santa Fe, New Mexico.

Societal norms: What people consider proper or acceptable in a certain period.

Speak her mind: An old-fashioned term meaning to say what you mean out loud.

Summit: The top of a mountain.

Sultry: Weather that is very hot and humid.

Underground Railroad: A network of secret routes and houses used by enslaved African Americans to escape into free states and Canada.

References

Birney, A. (2012). Julia Archibald Holmes, Santa Fe Trail Sojourner. Wagon Tracks, 26(4), (pages 17-20).

Colorado Women's Hall of Fame. (2014). Julia Archibald-Holmes. Retrieved from https://www.cogreatwomen.org/project/julia-archibald-holmes/

Julia Archibald Holmes. Santa Fe Historic Trail. Retrieved from the National Park Service. https://www.nps.gov/people/julia-archibald-holmes.htm

Shirley, Gayle & Wommack, Linda. (2023). Remarkable Colorado Women (3rd edition). Rowan & Littlefield Publishing Group, Inc. (pages 15-22).

About the Author

Clarissa (Chrissy) Willis is the product of a minister and a drama teacher. She has always had an active imagination and enjoys speaking and writing. She's lived in nine states. She was a major corporation's senior vice president of publishing and has been an educator for over 40 years. As a child growing up in Little Rock, Arkansas, she wrote stories and got into trouble for a variety of mishaps, from the attempted murder of her brother, a crime she swears wasn't her fault, to robbing the collection plate at church.

She earned a PhD in Early Childhood Special Education from the University of Southern Mississippi. In her professional life, Dr. Willis has provided workshops and keynote addresses in all 50 states and three foreign countries. She is a professor emeritus from the University of Sothern Indiana. Clarissa has written curricula for Frog Street Press, Kaplan Early Learning Company, and Scholastic. She has authored nineteen teacher resource books, including the award-winning Teaching Young Children with Autism Spectrum Disorder. In addition, she has written four children's books and is working on a memoir.

In her spare time, she serves on the board for Ozark Creative Writers, Between the Pages Writers Conference, and the Missouri Writers' Guild. She lives with her dog, George Maurice, in the Ozark Mountains of Northwest Arkansas. You can contact her at clarissa@clarissawillis.com.

About the Illustrator

Armand Hayes is an accomplished illustrator with a passion for comics, fantasy, and fairy tales. His artistic style is a blend of intricate details and vibrant colors, drawing readers into magical realms filled with fantastical creatures and whimsical characters.

He is a lifelong artist with a broad portfolio that ranges from corporate brand identity to children's artwork. With a heart full of wonder and a mind full of creativity, Armand is thrilled to share his passion for illustration with young readers everywhere. Through his artwork, he hopes to inspire curiosity, kindness, and an enduring love for storytelling.

When he's not busy illustrating, Armand enjoys running and making memories with his wife and young daughter in his hometown of Cleveland, Ohio.

Milton Keynes UK
Ingram Content Group UK Ltd.
UKRC030855301024
450402UK00013B/118

9 781959 548706